WILL MY PET GO TO HEAVEN?

WILL MY PET GO TO HEAVEN?

Please note that Destiny Image's publishing style capitalizes certain pronouns in Scripture that refer to the Father, Son, and Holy Spirit, and may differ from some publishers' styles. Take note that the name satan and related names are not capitalized. We choose not to acknowledge him, even to the point of violating grammatical rules.

Writers: Shae Cooke, Tammy Fitzgerald, Donna Scuderi,
Angela Rickabaugh Shears
Page layout: Dominique Abney

Ambient
An Imprint of Destiny Image

This book and all other Destiny Image, Revival Press, MercyPlace, Fresh Bread, Destiny Image Fiction, and Treasure House books are available at Christian bookstores and distributors worldwide.

ISBN 13 TP: 978-0-7684-3282-4
ISBN 13 HC: 978-0-7684-3509-2
ISBN 13 LP: 978-0-7684-3510-8
ISBN 13 Ebook: 978-0-7684-9087-9

For Worldwide Distribution, Printed in the U.S.A.
1 2 3 4 5 6 7 / 15 14 13 12 11 10

Contents

Introduction

Let the waters and the earth bring forth the living creatures...and God saw that it was good (see Genesis 1:20,24-25).

God created the living creatures before He created humankind. There is no doubt that He enjoyed the "great whales," "winged fowl," "cattle, and creeping thing, and beast of the earth" because He "saw that it was good." Next He created "man in Our image," so of course we, too, saw that the animals were good.

Pets have been welcomed into our lives as long ago as ancient Romans taming dogs and birds and Buddhist monks in China being entertained by ornamental goldfish, and of course,

we can't forget the infamous pet cats of the European Middle Ages that were destroyed because of witchcraft paranoia.

Today, in addition to thousands of traditional and new breeds of dogs and cats, there are guinea pigs, hamsters, parrots, cockatiels, frogs, turtles, and lizards that make their homes within our homes. It's not uncommon to read articles reporting that a dog or cat, or even a bird, saved a person from harm. Are these acts flukes—or are they intentional acts of life-saving kindness?

From Mark Twain's many beloved cats to Michael Jackson's chimp and Paris Hilton's fashion-accessory tiny Chihuahua, pets bring "meaning" to people in a variety of ways. Back in the 1950s when poodles were dyed to match an adoring owner's clothes or purse. Yikes!

Pets also get presidential status when living in the White House. Currently, Bo, President Obama's Portuguese water dog, is enjoying life as the "First Pet." President George W. Bush's Scottish Terriers, Miss Beazley and Barney, gave tours of the White House in their very own Internet video. A quick Web search reveals that United States Presidents back to Dwight D. Eisenhower had pets while holding office. John F. Kennedy had the most, including dogs, cats, ponies, parakeets, a rabbit, horse, and a canary named Robin. Go figure.

Entertainment businesses have been cashing in on animal and pet-inspired movies, magazines, and books for decades. Who doesn't love *Babe, My Dog Skip, Flipper, That Darn Cat,*

The Yearling, Lassie Come Home, 101 Dalmatians, and *Stuart Little?* Who didn't laugh at *Must Love Dogs* and *Beethoven* and cry at *Old Yeller* and *Bambi*? *Jaws* and *King Kong* evoke memories all their own.

Magazines and Internet Websites cater to pet lovers and range from how to: train, groom, show, feed, keep them healthy, and travel with them. From the childhood favorite magazine *Ranger Rick* to *Dog World, Cat Fancy, Bird Talk, Reptiles, Young Rider,* and *Hobby Farms,* there is advice, recommendations—and gimmicks—for every animal caretaker, including "Pet Sitters and Walkers," which have become lucrative careers or part-time employment opportunities for many.

The most famous "great whale" book is, of course, *Moby Dick.* And although Moby Dick wasn't Ahab's pet, they had a bond that went beyond the natural. A recent book by a "world famous psychic" purports that *All Pets Go to Heaven.* True? We explore all possibilities.

Most people hold a special place in their hearts for that first pet...and the last pet. At what point do people decide that the love they share with their pet isn't worth the pain of parting? As we delve into this personally heart-touching and gut-wrenching topic, we present many different perspectives and opinions, some relevant Scripture, and reflective *paws* for God's special creation.

Chapter 1

Of Mice and Marmaduke

Angela

The headline jumped off the computer screen at me, "Cat predicts 50 deaths in RI nursing home."[1] What? I read the article. I always read articles about dogs saving people from fires, birds waking a person in danger, a deer crashing through a beauty salon window in the middle of town—and how about the U.S. Marine who cared for that half-starved dog in the war zone and then brought him back to the States? Heartwarming and intriguing stories of the relationship that I believe God created between people and animals always catch my attention. Well, *some* animals. I would be *very* happy if there were no, none, zilch, nada snakes on the entire earth *or* in Heaven! They really freak me out. Hubby too.

Anyway, back to the article. Five-year-old Oscar was adopted as a kitten by a nursing and rehabilitation center in Providence, Rhode Island. Oscar "spends its days pacing from room to room, rarely spending any time with patients except those with just hours to live. When nurses once placed the cat on the bed of a patient they thought close to death, Oscar 'charged out' and went to sit beside someone in another room. The cat's judgment was better than that of the nurses; the second patient died that evening, while the first lived for two more days." Dr. David Dosa, a geriatrician and assistant professor at Brown University, first documented Oscar's gift in the *New England Journal of Medicine* in 2007. "Since then, the cat has gone on to double the number of imminent deaths it has sensed and convinced the geriatrician that it is no fluke." The article goes on to say that relatives and friends of the patients have been "comforted" knowing that the cat was with their loved ones when death came.

No doubt the patients felt the warmth of a furry friend next to them, one the Creator sent to help ease the transition from this world to the next. The center cares for people with severe dementia, so their minds have been altered over the years by the disease, but the rhythmic purring of a cat curled up beside them during the last few hours on earth would no doubt gently touch them in another part of their beings.

Our conversation about whether or not pets go to Heaven will be full of opinions...because we really won't know until we get there if our special friends will greet us. Until then, I love how Oscar helps usher these dear people from one kibbles

and bits life to another without saying a word, just doing what comes naturally. Surely God knew that even though He gave Adam a helpmate in Eve, people aren't always the best companions. At certain times, only a Fido, a Tweety, or an Oscar can comfort a scared soul or rejoice with a soaring spirit.

Shae

Then God made the beasts...and among them, Gracie, my zippy Jack Russell ~~Terror~~ Terrier...and God proclaimed that it was "good." Later He said, "Have dominion over it," and the heavenly host burst forth in ~~feather-fluffing guffaw~~ song, and the dog thought, *No problem...my new master is trainable.* Yea though I walk through the valley of the shadow of a domineering bouncy yo-yo....

If I could just bottle Gracie's energy—take a shot of JRT—I could run 10K, rewrite *War and Peace,* and pick up after my son, all before breakfast! How our Creator God could put such tightly coiled springs into such little legs is beyond me! If a group of unicorns is called a "blessing," twelve or more cows a "flink," a group of frogs an "army," a group of rhinos a "crash," a group of geese a "gaggle," a group of larks an "exaltation," a group of owls a "parliament," and a group of ravens a "murder," then a group of JRTs has to be a "pandemonium!"

It is this very bundle of intelligent sheer mania that has seen my son and I through tough times in my sudden singleness,

and this is where I relate to your comments, Angela, about the comfort a pet can bring. Gracie's arrival five years ago into our home as a puppy helped us shift our focus off sadness and onto her precocious antics. In addition, she has taught me much about overlooking the little annoying things that rob us of joy, like poop (or snot) on the carpet. I guess that is why I named her Grace, that and because she does remind me of the loveable Gracie Allen. And because she will, on signal, put her paws together to pray…for treats of course…and (brag-brag) she also rolls over, plays dead, high-fives, waves, shakes a paw, break dances, rides a roller blade, knows her left paw from the right, jumps through hoops, fetches magazines, and speaks.

Point to a tree trunk and say, "What's that?"

"Bark! Bark!"

Ask her how she is feeling, and she answers, "Ruff!"

She's smart I tell you!

Please don't ask me how I found time to train up my child, too! *rolling hazel eyes heavenward!*

Job himself, in his sorry plight, said, *"But ask the animals, and they will teach you…in* [God's] *hand is the life of every living thing and the breath of every human being"* (Job 12:7 NRSV). I'm persuaded that God created animals to teach us more about God's breath in us and what it means to be divinely human—exemplifying forgiveness and unconditional love, loyalty and

courage, and other essential qualities that we can apply to our lives here and in Heaven. Moreover, and this is important for all ages, they help us learn to play, yes play for play's sake—no winners or losers, no domination or competition, no mean coaches or taunters; just feel-good romps, frolics, and tussles to bring laughter (and youth) back into our days!

Sounds like Heaven to me!

Donna

Where to begin? Hopefully not with Skippy, the pup my parents adopted when I was two-ish. Poor fella. The unwitting canine toilet bungee jumper. The cord was his wiry white tail, and you can guess who was at the other end of it.

"Donna!" my mother cried. "What are you doing?"

"I'm giving Skippy a bath," I replied as the traumatized canine shook his soaking face and gasped for air.

"Honey, we don't bathe puppies upside down in—in *there.* Here, let's give him a new bath together."

Fade to bathtub.

If Skippy had known what that day had in store, he would

surely have chosen the mean streets of Bushwick to the cozy confines and reliable cuisine found in the ground-floor flat on Linden Street.

Man, I loved that dog. And, yes, I do remember when I was two. Crazy, right? Although, I will grant you, the incident was not caught on nanny-cam and the dialogue has been reconstructed to the best of my ability. What I don't remember is what became of Skippy. Seems like he was there one day and gone the next. I wonder if he requested a transfer. Or worse, was rescued by an ASPCA SWAT team with intelligence on my dog-dunking ways—although I probably would have remembered the latter.

But I digress. The good news is (someone please let PETA know) that I quickly learned how to express my love for animals more appropriately. Dear, faithful, Rusty Boy (who lived to be 18) would attest to that. So would Cherry Baby, the six-and-seven-toed cat who curled up beside my ailing mother and stayed there for Mom's final hours. As for Buckwheat and Miss Crabtree, my little rascal girls who shared my life and home for 15 years—they were doted over, too. Those lovable purr-balls made life so much sweeter for their presence.

So Angela, I also read the story of Oscar and the nursing home, and I can't help but marvel at how the plan of creation plays out each day. Oscar has some kind of instinct built into his cat-ness that, as far as I'm concerned, had to have been "factory-installed." Some would argue that Oscar and his forebears learned how to behave over eons of time. The fact remains,

IMHO, that it started somewhere with the Adam of Oscars. That's a can of worms for another day. The amazing thing I think all people can agree upon is this: people and their pets have an affinity that precedes them. One trip to the pound makes that clear. Those dear, homeless four-footed characters stand up and applaud at the mere scent of a human. I'm pretty sure the Creator has everything to do with that.

Tammy

Ah, the bond between a pet and his or her human! Do any of you remember the beginning of Disney's original *101 Dalmatians?* It's absolutely classic: The dog, Pongo, lazing in his flat with his "pet," Roger, narrates his contemplative evaluation of his human and concludes that it's about time he found a "mate" for Roger. Window-shopping the "breeds" (from his own window, LOL), Pongo observes a whole lineup of dogs and their people—all hilariously matched in appearance. Oh, the good old days of quiet, subtle, visual wit!

It's an old joke, but it keeps on proving itself true just often enough to stay funny. I can personally testify to having seen a few striking examples of people looking very much like their cat or dog (or parakeet!). I just hope I don't end up looking like my own ball of fluff, Kitty. Even if he *is* the prettiest cat I've ever "served"!

Just kidding. ^_^ Actually, of all the cats I've ever met, Kitty is one of the least aloof and demanding felines in the world,

IMHO. He is a calm old fellow who loves to cuddle and be around people. Maybe it's because he's been absolutely adored to pieces since the day he wandered down our street and was picked up by yours truly, 12 years old and lonesome for a best friend. I still maintain to this day that Kitty has a people-loving personality simply because he's been so *loved* by people.

Animals are like little children in this—both are extremely teachable "sponges." Now maybe not all animals will learn what we *want* them to, but I believe that any animal that spends a lot of time around humans is going to learn, even if we weren't intending to teach them! To quote *Les Misérables* by Victor Hugo, "Animals are nothing but the portrayal of our virtues and vices made manifest to our eyes, the visible reflections of our souls. God displays them to us to give us food for thought." I couldn't agree more! Animals reflect the attributes they've been exposed to—whether they've been loved, ignored, or tragically abused.

In the homes of people who love and serve the Lord and each other, I've only ever met *good* pets. Sure, the dog may be a little excitable (some things just come down to breed), and the cat may take awhile to warm up to you. We all have different opinions about what makes a truly "good" pet—and our opinions may be a bit different at four in the morning! But I'll tell you—just from my own experience—I've seen some animals that qualified as truly "mean-spirited" creatures. It can happen. But I've never seen pets like those in households filled with the Lord's peace and love.

Call it a small example of *"glorious freedom"* (see Rom. 8:19-21 NIV). Or glorious fuzzdom!

Endnote

1. Tom Leonard, "Cat predicts 50 deaths in RI nursing home," *Telegraph.co.uk,* February 1, 2010.

Your Reflections

Your Reflections

Your Reflections

Your Reflections

Your Reflections

Chapter 2

Nearer My Dog to Thee

Angela

For many years I just could *not* understand "dog people." Hubby and I would (politely and discreetly, of course) snicker and shake our heads when we saw people walking their dogs and then stooping to pick up poop. Yuck! We'd poo-poo those who spent hundreds of dollars on gourmet food, vet bills, and salon visits for their pets. And to have their dog sleep in bed with them? How ludicrous! Maybe growing up in a rural community made us think that animals were more for scaring away intruders (or anything that moved) while being tied to a little doghouse in the back yard, or for consuming—think Outback, KFC, Kraft American Cheese....

Growing up, my older and only sister, Julianne, had a dog, Tammy; and for a few years I had a cat, Francie. One sunny summer day when I was 5, a little adorable all-black kitten emerged from a cornfield next to Aunt Louise's house. I just "had" to save this little fur ball, "Can't I *please* take her home?!" My mother gave in after much whining and wailing (something I've since perfected—just ask Hubby). Tammy and Francie were both "outside" pets—when I was outside, I paid attention to them. Other than that, my dear mom and dad tended to both. Typical.

While growing my own children, I gave in to a variety of pets ranging from fish to cats to dogs. I kept them all at arm's length—peripheral parts of family life. Today, my eldest daughter Andria declared her home a "pet-free zone" after a few failed attempts to get used to having a litter box in her beautifully detailed and sparkling clean home. She recently compromised with a gerbil who lives out of sight in the boys' bedroom.

After a few empty-nest years, three of which were spent living in Hawaii, I drove by a sign that periodically appeared along the road near our home "SHAGGY DOG pups for sale." You know that feeling when you know that you're going to give in even though you go through the motion of trying to talk yourself out of something? Well, a few days later, we were knocking at the door and then picking out the cutest, most adorable Old English sheepdog that God ever created. Margaret Thatcher (Maggie for short) has been spoiled by us for the past seven years. Yes, we pick up her poop, and spend hundreds

of dollars a year at the doggy salon, and yes, all 80 plus pounds of her sleeps smack dab between us in bed every night!

Will Maggie be looking for me with her one big blue eye and one big brown eye at the pearly gates and wagging her little stubby tail when she sees me? Maybe. After all John writes, *"Now I saw heaven opened, and behold, a white horse..."* (Rev. 19:11). Is this white horse a pet of *"the one called Faithful and True,"* or perhaps the pet of a person who mourned its passing? Hmmm...

Shae

Tell me Angela, what does having Margaret Thatcher sleeping between you and your husband "every night" *not* do for your love life? LOL. I think I'm glad to see you have become a pet convert. *grin*

Gracie sleeps at the *foot* of my bed, facing the door, in protective mode, listening for things that go "bump" in the night. One night in the wee hours, something crashed against the front door of my home. Yikes! My 10-inch high, 13-pound pooch went berserk, putting her nose to the ground under the crack, fearlessly clawing, sniffing, growling, frantically trying to get at whatever it was on the other side. No bones about it, with that sniffer, she knew what lurked there. Nonetheless, I was thinking *intruder* (there had been a rash of home invasions) and ran to my son's room (his window is right there) and

shone a flashlight onto the patio. Bear! Four bears at that. What a relief! (In truth, I fear humans more than I do wildlife). My patio is small, and with that many bears on it trying to access my albeit empty garbage container, they couldn't help but press against the door as they maneuvered their plan. Come morning, I found that they had hauled it up the stairs and rolled the can across the acre lawn. The claw marks are on the lid to prove it! Ever since that incident, Gracie intuitively stays by the front door, nose to the ground until she is certain all is well.

As a little girl, my favorite hymns always involved animals and creation and their connection to Creator God, which connects them to His children. "All Things Bright and Beautiful"[1] and "God Sees the Little Sparrow Fall"[2] still resonate deeply. Animals, I believe, generally are *wired* to have a constant awareness of God and likely communicate with Him instinctively; they inherently know His awareness of them; they know His existence as their Creator. Their brains just do not work in the same way that ours do as much as we like to think. I wouldn't think that they question God's existence or argue His ways or feel they need to improve on or change what God has already made good and perfect. I mean, how many poodles do you know that have had boob jobs (now that would be expensive with eight boobies!). I venture animals (and I'm not sure about fish, reptiles, and bugs) know God without even thinking about it, without trying to explain it, and without putting Him in a box. They simply know and accept that they are created creatures beloved enough of God that He would deem them worthy of creating each uniquely and of saving with humankind at

the time of the Flood and of being frequently referred to in His Word from the beginning to the end of time.

Thank goodness God made animals beautifully different. They lack human reasoning, perhaps premeditation, and many of our more complicated emotions, but have unique and special abilities, such as a propensity to feel one another's emotions more than humans have. While we get caught up in our day-to-day lives, worried about tomorrow and how big and high ~~my~~ our boobs are (thus completely missing today), they live the day in its fullness, enjoying the journey. They also seem to know their place in creation more than we do—that is until we come along and dress them up in leather Harley jackets, push up bras, or Gucci tutus.

Donna

Angela, you can get a witness right here and now—I haven't seen the "Pups for Sale" sign along the roadside yet, but it's a matter of time until the rule of this roost is turned over to a dachshund. I've resisted for a long time, but there's only so much practicality a Mediterranean type from New York City can muster. A soul can live without dog love only so long—and it has been soooooo long.

Picture this heavenly scene: the sausage-shaped sheer muscle of a weiner dog body wiggling at the front door and yipping as I haul in the groceries. Brown pleading eyes beg as dog brow

pitches upward. Long auburn snout pokes into sacks of foodstuffs, sniffing for snacks or a brand-new bone. In the middle of the pantry restock is the usual tripping over the four-legged, low-lying, living hot dog wending its way between my feet. "Stop some more!" I plead before plunging headlong into the countertop, hoping for something with a hardness level of less than ten to break my fall.

After the ER visit and application of a fine new ankle cast in my choice of fashion colors, those dangerous little canine legs attempt to launch into bed and snuggle next to the plaster accoutrement lurking under the comforter. All is forgiven, and I kiss the bridge of his silken snout. I doze peacefully, knowing that if anything smashes into the front door during the night (at my house or Shae's!), my fearless redhead will raise the moat (his bark) and give a large helping of what for to the disturbers of the peace.

Later on, oh say around 4 A.M., the pitter patter of tiny paws follows me to the—well—you know—the place everyone goes in the middle of the night. Pets of singles demand certain liberties, of course. My cats sure did. Forget about closing the—uh, you know which door. Unacceptable! Buckwheat and Miss Crabtree would stick their forelegs under the door, pads turned upward and reaching, reaching until it looked like their little bones would snap in two. Unacceptable! Come on in, girls. Join the party in the—well, you get the idea.

I'm not sure whether my elongated friend and I will meet up in Heaven. I doubt that he'd be worried about it. The Bible

doesn't say God made weiner dogs in His image and likeness, after all. But, for sure, He made them with people in mind. God knew that crazy-looking little guy would paste a smile on the face of anyone who laid eyes on him. And He knew that the energizer hot dog and the human would share a forever bond.

Just imagining it all is a little piece of Heaven.

Tammy

Sometimes I watch my darling little fluff of a cat and wonder, *Can he see things that I can't?* Is the spirit realm open to the eyes of animals, and is Kitty nonchalantly parading around my house, indifferent to both angels and humans alike? It's something I ponder when I remember Balaam's donkey (see Num. 22:21-28). I find it interesting that God opened the donkey's *mouth*, but it doesn't say his eyes needed any help. The donkey saw the angel, presumably all on his own. (I guess donkeys eat a lot more carrots than we do...LOL.)

> *For [even the whole] creation (all nature) waits expectantly and longs earnestly for God's sons to be made known [waits for the revealing, the disclosing of their sonship]. For the creation (nature) was subjected to frailty (to futility, condemned to frustration), not because of some intentional fault on its part, but by the will of Him Who so subjected it—[yet] with the hope that nature*

> *(creation) itself will be set free from its bondage to decay and corruption [and gain an entrance] into the glorious freedom of God's children. We know that the whole creation [of irrational creatures] has been moaning together in the pains of labor until now* (Romans 8:19-22 AMP).

Romans is a great book for puzzlers! I won't pretend to completely understand or be able to interpret this, but one thing seems strongly implied to me—"irrational creatures" know *something* that is often hidden from us two-leggers. Somehow animals and all of nature seem to be aware of their fallen condition, yet they are not the ones who have been offered Christ's redemption. That's for the "made in His image" set!

I wonder if there's some inexplicable spiritual sense that animals have that makes them long for the Lord's final triumph. Sometimes I'm really curious just how much they *know*, you know? Animals can have the most amazing instincts about the weather, danger, food, and people. I wonder if maybe, on some very intangible level, my cat shares in this "frustration" and "waits expectantly" for every step I take in my walk with the Lord.

Hey, call me crazy (you wouldn't be the first), but isn't it kind of fun to imagine your pets as a little furry cheering squad, delighting in your relationship with the Father and rejoicing in your growth in Him? Come on Angela, I've met Maggie, and she doesn't even need the pom-poms—she practically *is* one! ^_^

Endnotes

1. Cecil F. Alexander, "All Things Bright and Beautiful," *Hymns for Little Children* (1848).

2. Maria Strobe, "God Sees the Little Sparrow Fall" (1874).

Your Reflections

Your Reflections

Your Reflections

Your Reflections

Your Reflections

Chapter 3

Piddler on the Roof

Donna

Piddlers. Buckwheat—my perfect feline friend in every way but this one—had the most unique penchant for piddling. She was litter box savvy, but found a pastime that involved serial piddling of a high order. I mean, this manx-looking master had some kind of routine! It drove me to distraction for a couple of months, and then it was over—I mean *over,* and not because the Mistress of the House successfully enforced the rules. No, this was a Buckwheat-ordained project of limited duration. When the project was complete, the piddling stopped.

I've yet to understand the primal side of this calculated act of household terror, but here's how it went: Not long after

adopting Buckwheat and Miss Crabtree, I redecorated the living room. "What were you thinking?!" you ask. Well, I can't say for sure. I bought this neat rattan-framed sofa with a brick-on-beige frond kind of pattern and 12 upholstery buttons (two rows of six buttons each) sewn into the one-piece seat cushion. One day, I noticed a wet spot around Button Number One. *Hmmm,* I thought, *wonder where that came from.*

A few days later, Button Number Two, just to the right of Button Number One, was soaked. "Aha! Feline shenanigans!" I cried after a revelatory sniff test. Looking at my two darlings with as stern a motherly glare as I could summon, I declared, "Somebody better fess up—and quick!"

Yeah, right.

Then one evening, I walked into the living room to find sweet, precious Buckwheat in a classic litter box squat, filling up the indentation surrounding Button Number Three. "Busted!" screamed her eyes as she shot past me like a cat out of hell, ears back and black eyes a-poppin.

I was furious. My brand-new couch was ruined, far as I could tell. And the war was not nearly over. There were nine more buttons to go. Buckwheat missed nary a one. She worked them, literally in order (what was *that* about?) until all 12 buttons were Buckwheated. Mission accomplished! Fait accompli! Magnifico! Not.

As bummed as I was about the sofa, I never had a second

thought about my buddy Buckwheat. A sofa is a sofa, but 'Wheatie and I, we were kindred spirits. Don't draw any New Age inferences from that. We were *divinely* connected. There was nothing within my power that I wouldn't do or give to care for and love those cats. I loved buying their favorite toys and playing their favorite games. I loved keeping them healthy and spry. They were God's gift, without a doubt. As for 'Wheatie and the buttons, she never piddled again until she was 15 years old and ailing.

I miss those girls to this day. If nothing else, the memory of them will be with me in Heaven.

Angela

LOL! Dear, dear, Donna, I'm not laughing *at* you, I'm laughing (or weeping) *with* you! We had a male cat once that made the mistake of leaving his (horribly stinky) mark in the house years ago. He was promptly taken to my cousin's farm where he lived happily *outside* for many chasing-mice days until he went to…

My brother, Ronn, (who raised Siberian Husky show dogs) sent me one of those forwarded chain message type of emails the other day (as is his custom about once a week), and I just have to share it. It's just a fun smiley bit of humor—no offense intended to the original Genesis account.

Adam and Eve said, "Lord, when we were in the garden, You walked with us every day. Now we do not see You anymore. We are lonesome here, and it is difficult for us to remember how much You love us."

And God said, "I will create a companion for you that will be with you and that will be a reflection of My love for you, so that you will love Me even when you cannot see me. Regardless of how selfish or childish or unlovable you may be, this new companion will accept you as you are and will love you as I do, in spite of yourselves."

And God created a new animal to be a companion for Adam and Eve.

And it was a good animal.

And God was pleased.

And the new animal was pleased to be with Adam and Eve, and he wagged his tail.

And Adam said, "Lord, I have already named all the animals in the Kingdom, and I cannot think of a name for this new animal."

And God said, "I have created this new animal to be a reflection of My love for you; his name will be a reflection of My own name, and you will call him DOG."

And Dog lived with Adam and Eve and was a companion to them and loved them.

And they were comforted.

And God was pleased.

And Dog was content and wagged his tail.

After awhile, it came to pass that an angel came to the Lord and said, "Lord, Adam and Eve have become filled with pride. They strut and preen like peacocks and they believe they are worthy of adoration. Dog has indeed taught them that they are loved, but perhaps too well."

And God said, "I will create for them a companion who will be with them and who will see them as they are. The companion will remind them of their limitations, so they will know that they are not always worthy of adoration."

And God created CAT to be a companion to Adam and Eve.

And Cat would not obey them. And when Adam and Eve gazed into Cat's eyes, they were reminded that they were not supreme beings.

And Adam and Eve learned humility.

And they were greatly improved.

Hmmm...it may be time for hubby and I to get a cat... or two.

Shae

Well, I wish Gracie would improve. For all her tricks, she still piddles and poops when she feels like it, and try as I have, I cannot re-steer her strong-willed penchant for carpets. I mean, why not the kitchen floor, better yet, the bathroom? "Tile girl, t-i-l-e." I've heard that some cats and dogs know how to use human potties. I hope for her sake, that she does learn to flush; otherwise she'll have a date at the Rainbow Bridge with her Maker, if you know what I mean. Only kidding—I would never harm a hair on her dreadlocked head or hurt anything on two or four legs. I draw the line, however, at mucho-legged beasties: spiders, centipedes, and...do houseflies and mosquitos have limbs? Ditto for anything that slithers or hisses. OK, add to my list hyenas, wild boars, rats, and the three mice that moved into my car for a winter to spring "partay."

Can you say, Snap! Snap! Snap! Ouch. I have to admit not enjoying the sight of their broken little necks. Oh, but the alternative was horrible: slow death by poison and the (gag) potential odiferous aftermath. What's a girl, a blonde one at that, who lives atop a mountain and has to get to the Prada sale, to do when advised, "Get rid of them thar varmints before they chew the brake lines."

I love God's creatures and appreciate that God has each one here for a reason, and honestly, I do steward His creation as well as I can. There are times, however, when I have to seek deeper revelation concerning certain ones, like snakes. "I mean, Lord, do You love them?" I guess if I look deeper, I have difficulty wrapping my head around that first Genesis image of the devil, seared in my mind as ugly to the core. Then again, there is such a thing as the face that only a mother (or Father?) could love; and the Word does say that He is loving toward all He has made (see Ps. 145:9,13,16-17).

I don't know that we Christians are as loving toward or do as good a job in creation stewardship as the many non-Christians have who have diligently worked to preserve creation's wonder, beauty, and integrity. In his book *Biology Through the Eyes of Faith,*[1] emeritus professor of biology Richard Wright references what he terms "the Cyrus Principle," the process by which God often uses unbelievers to accomplish His purposes. Pop philosopher and Pastor Francis Schemer in *Pollution and the Death of Man*[2] sided with the 1960s hippies citing the Church as both complicit in its lack of care for God's creation and negligent in its teaching on the theology of nature. Ouch Chihuahua, it stings and shouts truth. Certainly, my lifetime has seen the loss of much wildlife habitat and the extinction, or its threat, of many species. "Lost Animals of the 20th Century," a documentary series shown on the Discovery Channel in the 1990s, covered the demise of several. Do you know that some became extinct for being too charismatic? I wonder if there is such a thing as being too pee-matic? For Gracie's sake, I pray not. I

also wonder, *Will there be toilets in Heaven?* Perhaps fodder for another discussion!

Tammy

If there's one thing that must be the indoor/outdoor deal-breaker for every pet owner, it'd be piddling. If a dog can hold her water or a cat can learn to use his litter box—welcome to our home. If not—welcome to our yard! ^_^

When I was little we had two outdoor cats—males that came to us too late for training. After they passed on, a new little kitten wandered down the street and stopped at our door. I don't remember why this one got the OK for indoor living, but I do remember attempting to convey to his fluffy little mind the mystical purposes of this plastic tray full of sand. I'd hold his paw and scratch the litter for him, trying to teach him to "cover up" with little piles. He'd try to reclaim his paw with a disgruntled look.

After much patience and practice in my high calling of stewarding my puffball of creation, the lesson was learned—sort of. Kitty got the concept of the box, and he picked up on scratching at the litter, he just didn't *quite* figure out what the scratching was *for*. The end result—he's indoor/outdoor. He uses his box, but we prefer to let him out because he throws the litter *out* of the box in all directions whenever he uses it.

Apparently the floor needs more coverage than the "deposits" in the litter box, in his mind!

Here's some "pet food for thought," àla C.S. Lewis: "The personality of the tame animals is largely the gift of man—that their mere sentience is reborn to soulhood in us as our mere soulhood is reborn to spirituality in Christ."[3] In other words:

> To Lewis the practice of taming animals, and making them more humanlike, was an obvious parallel to God's way of making believing Christians more Christ-like. He suggested that domestic animals might somehow achieve immortality in the context of their masters' immortality. It is a comforting thought for anyone who has hoped to see their beloved pet in heaven, though not much use to a dog belonging to a non-Christian.[4]

Haha, touché. But from where I sit—on my cat-hair-covered couch—it's good enough for me. If there ever *was* any sort of possible redemption for fallen Creation, what else could it be but a devoted relationship with a loving master? Talk about a picture of us and Christ! Sign me up for obedience training; it's a dog's life, and I could take a few lessons from self-abandoned adoration like that!

Endnotes

1. Richard Wright, *Biology Through the Eyes of Faith* (San Francisco, CA: HarperOne, 1989).

2. Francis Schemer, *Pollution and the Death of Man* (Cross Stream, IL: Tyndale House/1970; Crossway Books/1992).

3. C.S. Lewis, *The Problem of Pain* (San Francisco, CA: Harper, 2001), 145-146.

4. "Christianity: C.S. Lewis," BBC, Pet Heaven, http://www.bbc.co.uk/religion/religions/christianity/people/cslewis_1.shtml (accessed February 17, 2010).

Your Reflections

Your Reflections

Your Reflections

Your Reflections

Your Reflections

Chapter 4

Thou Shalt Have No Pets Before Me

Donna

Picture it: 1979-ish. I'm living in a small one-bedroom apartment in Queens, NYC. 'Wheatie and the incomparable Miss Crabtree have been my roomies for some time. They have just gotten to the point (after neutering) where there isn't always one of them in heat and ready to tear the other to shreds. A feline visitor turns up in the hallway between the outer door that doesn't lock and the inner door that does (but isn't worth a whit of security). Said visitor is quite young and female. She's in good shape and has a collar, but no I.D. She can't have traveled far; humans barely make it across Grand Avenue without getting smushed. I serve up a feast fit for a kitty and begin my search for a newspaper ad or bulletin board post that describes

her. No luck. I put up posters around the hood. No response. Finally, I go knocking on doors, with my forlorn friend in a carrier. There are thousands of families within blocks of my flat. I am determined to find the poor soul who is looking for this cutie. Failure is not an option; a third cat is not an option for me and the girls.

Within 30 minutes of canvassing, I knock on the right door. An elderly woman cries out, "Oh, my Misty! [Or was it Molly?] You had me so worried."

Misty responds, "Meoooooww, Mommy." (OK, don't quote me on that.)

Suddenly, I am overcome with the aroma of multiple cat-ness. I almost gag, but hold my lunch as I realize that Misty belongs to a "cat lady." Cats stream toward the door from inside, and I wonder what I should do. Then it dawns on me: the cats look to be in terrific shape. It's this dear woman and her home that need rescuing. She obviously has issues (welcome to the club).

I hand over the purring Misty and suspend judgment.

Angela

I can honestly say that I've never put a pet before my God, family, nation, or my favorite television show (Monk) for that

matter. But these days, there are many (believers and non-believers) who put, um, gee, football, NASCAR, or a too-fun Saturday night before going to church, their career before family time, and their political tradition before pledging allegiance to the most free and generous country on earth.

We all have idols of some sort—some are just more easily identified than others. I doubt many Americans have a "graven image" sitting on their mantle or "gods" lining their closets, but how many have prized trophies on the mantle and/or designer stuff in their closets? (Not counting Shae's shoe closet, of course.) All Christians are served up a dish of guilt over enjoying things a bit "too much." Where does appreciating God's gifts stop and idolizing stuff start? Have pet owners crossed the line when they serve their pets gourmet dog food (Maggie gets good ol' Purina), spend hard-earned money on expensive surgeries or treatments (none yet), or take them to the salon for an all-day primping package (guilty as charged) for their pets? Are we idolizing or just taking care of furry or feathered friends?

In my opinion, the people who idolize animals are PETA and some over-the-top Green Peacers who hold extreme views. Remember when PETA griped when President Obama swiped at a fly during a press conference? Good grief. And when two PETA-heads showed up at the Westminster Dog Show in February 2010 with signs whining about something or other? Of course animals should be treated with kindness and should be taken care of, but to put them above their Creator is just plain silly.

I know two people who may be near the silly-tipping point, though. One friend, Shelley, has three poodles that received years of undivided attention, love, and total devotion. Then Shelley got married and the next year had an adorable baby boy. Her three four-legged "guys" have now resorted to piddling wherever and whenever in revolt. Another dear friend, Shirley, wrote to me recently:

> My pet rabbit, Cookie, is a constant source of joy and laughter. Cookie is a good-sized bunny, weighing in at 10 lbs or so. She is litter trained and lives primarily in my bedroom, which is "bunny proofed." Every morning when my feet hit the floor, she hops over to me eagerly awaiting her morning treat. When I arrive home from work in the evening and bring her salad (in her own personal Pfaltzgraff bowl), she gets so excited for that first bite of banana (her favorite!). God blessed us with these wonderful animal companions who give us so much and ask so little in return. I believe with all my heart that He has a special place for them when they leave this earth. I envision myself someday being in a beautiful garden surrounded by all of the precious animals I've been privileged to have in my life here on earth.

Another is a radio talk show host, Michael Savage. I must admit I'm hooked on his sometimes caustic monologues because his humor, stories, and outlook on life, politics, and the news is thought-provoking, unique, and entertaining. Savage has a tiny toy poodle, Teddy, that he talks about frequently.

This gruff, New York City-grown (Brooklyn, not Queens like Donna), UC Berkeley-educated man who is now transplanted in "San Franfreako" loves his little dog with such passion that it's hard not to relate and smile along.

Our Maggie is hubby and my best friend, but to idolize her—no, we take those "Big 10" that the Lord handed down seriously. Besides, she wouldn't want it that way.

Tammy

Here's a rousing "Ditto!" to that, Angela. Nobody can take Kitty's place in my heart, but his special spot doesn't come close to replacing Jesus. No crowding and no overlap either. And I don't *think* anyone would get suspicious from watching my behavior...or my spending on him!

It's a little incredible what some folks will spend on their pets. Now, don't get me wrong—while I feel no inclination to put human clothes on an animal, I don't particularly mind if some people choose to. Especially with some of those cute little lap dogs. But to spend upward of $200 for authentic historical period dresses in miniature? I just need to know one thing—*why?* Why the doll-sized Victorian gown? (And just out of curiosity, are the gowns more comfortable for doggies than their human versions? Because if not, we might really need PETA for once! LOL)

Without pointing fingers, let's just say I found this apparel for sale on a Website that also provided numerous other pet luxuries. Like $300 doggy beds in mahogany or bamboo, similarly-priced pet *strollers* (because I guess the little babies can't actually *walk* when you take them out for one), a $345 marble-topped, iron-legged table with inset food and water dishes, doggy nail polish (claw polish?), pet cologne, and little engraved stone memorials for the yard or garden—again, for only a couple hundred dollars. And of course, we all know about pet health insurance and the ever-incredible pet graveyards—easy ways to spend as much on your pet as you do on yourself or your children.

All this for everyday pet owners. I don't even want to think about the pampering some pets get—Paris Hilton isn't the only celebrity with a pet that probably eats better than half the people in the world.

Again, not trying to point fingers or sound judgmental. Goodness knows, with that kind of money, they could do worse things with it than lavish it on a chosen animal. And even we who are not starlets can probably justify some pet spending as either caring for God's creation or "just for fun." But I think it's worth a cautionary word and a second look at what we're doing. The "Thou shalts" aren't to be taken lightly, and whether we're spending as much on Rover's wardrobe as on our own (or more!) or even if we're not, it's always good to double-check our hearts. "Who's first in my heart, in my life, in my finances?" If we can't answer honestly, "Jesus!" but have to take a second look at Spot, it might be time to refocus on the one true God.

Jesus might not want you to buy Him a Victorian gown, though...just a heads-up. ^_^

Shae

Jesus would definitely not suit a bustle, and I agree about the seriousness of the "Thou shalts," and in particular, "Thou shalt not take the name of the Lord in vain." If I hear one more "Dog spelled backward is God," I'm gonna bark. Honestly, what are people thinking? "Did" spelled backward is still *did*—and to feline aficionados who desperately wish that T-A-C spells "God," a cat is a cat, and a bird is a bird, and God and only God is God, any way you spell their names or His! A divine line crossed is divine protection breached, and I won't be the one caught in the aftermath of the parting of the Red Sea, if you know what I mean.

Listen, I am "animal lover extraordinaire," and every dog, cat, bear, coyote, raccoon, newt, and hummingbird in the neighborhood knows that I'm a food source, a helping hand, and a warm shelter. Of course I adore and indulge my pets, but never over Father God in Heaven, the Creator of our universe, and never over humanity, which He prizes, and only sometimes over shoes, Angela, and only when they are on extreme sale, or slightly used, and that goes for Gracie's goodies too. Pet ownership is all about knowing and appreciating the order of the universe as God intended it and acting accordingly and responsibly because by and by dogs will have their day in Heaven. I'm

convinced they will be given free reign to romp and enjoy many benefits they don't receive here! I really do believe one day we will finally see pigs fly.

On a sadder note, in the aftermath of the Haitian disaster, most television channels around here (Canada) carried graphic telecasts of suffering, bleeding, maimed, disfigured, starving, and homeless men, women, and children. I recall one such telecast's station break: an emotionally charged appeal by a local major animal shelter for donations. The commercial, hosted by a well-known female singer, featured two long minutes of overly dramatic footage of forlorn looking animals *in their care.* The camera panned in on sorrowful looking eyes and turned up the volume on woeful mews and pitiful cries, and the songstress sang the saddest song I've ever heard in the background. I'm still hearing the haunting cries of children roaming the streets in search of their parents, and thinking, *Whoa, bad timing. At least the animals have shelter, medication, bandages, pain relief, food, water, but hundreds of thousands of human victims have not.* Then I thought *whoa* again, *How could anyone, as hard as it was to look at those suffering creatures, not pity the human victims of the quake more? Moreover, even consider sending money to the animal shelter over Haiti?* Hey, listen, I'm the first one to help an animal in distress, but Lord help us! I'm sure the people of Port au Prince did not prioritize their pets.

Sadly the reality is that many pets are abused, neglected, and hungry, and it is a shame, and we need to do something about it, but the well-being of humanity has to be prioritized

because among them are precious people, like Donna's cat lady, who do and will care for the animals.

God had beautiful reasons why He created Adam and Eve and why He created the animal kingdom *for us* and on the same day as us! It be-*hooves* (groan) us to cherish that kingly gift and to honor the fact that we are made in His image. As His children, we have a responsibility and the honor first to love and dote on Him as our Father and second to love and dote on each other. If we did those things as well as we should, there would be no guilt in overindulging our pets.

Now please excuse me while I call up the pet psychologist to help break the news to Gracie that she cannot have that day in the Dapper Dog Pet Spa soaking her toenails as I promised her.

Your Reflections

Your Reflections

Your Reflections

Your Reflections

Your Reflections

Chapter 5

What Pet Would Jesus Have?

Shae

If people can wreck kids, if we can turn each other bad, it stands to reason that we can wreck our animals as well. The devil too can turn people evil, thus yes, I believe there are bad animals, perhaps, even possessed, but through no fault of their own because they don't exercise reasoning, at least I don't think so!

I recall hearing a report put out by BBC World News in 2003 about the Malawi terror beast—a mysterious wild animal later identified as a possibly rabid hyena—that went on an extended killing craze. Get this. According to Wikipedia (not the most reliable source), this beast fatally attacked two elderly women and a 3-year-old child, crushed their skulls and ate their

intestines and genitals. Sorry for the graphic content. It also severely injured over a dozen others; some of the victims lost their legs, hands, eyes, and ears. Thousands of villagers from surrounding areas stampeded to a community hall for refuge. Witnesses reported this beast as identical to an animal responsible for the deaths of five people and the disfigurement of over 20 others the previous year. Trouble is, wildlife officials got that animal, shot it dead. The general belief was that this beast had come back to life to exact revenge. Ooooooh.

I have a parrot like that, although Wally, a Pacific Blue Parrotlet, goes for male fingers. (Parrotlets are also known as pocket parrots, and, averaging about 5 ounces in weight, they are the world's smallest, can speak up a storm, and live 20-35 years.) As it is with Jack Russells and other big personalities living in small bodies, the short man complex can kick in, and boy, Wally sure becomes powerful for his size. Combine that with what appears to be an unforgiving spirit toward my ex, who has to visit occasionally, and well, Wally does become devilish, depending on who's asking. Wally has angelic moments, though. You should hear his rendition of "Yes, Jesus Wuvs Me."

If there are any bad animals, we first have to separate what we think is bad from the natural predator-prey relationship of the animal kingdom and what we know as survival instinct. I'm thinking man-eating (scavengers aside) lions, crocodiles, piranhas, sharks, 5-inch high parrots, 10-inch high dogs, and the woman who sucker punched me for the one remaining 75 percent off Coach purse at the wholesale outlet. She's right up there with the hyena. (Forgive me, Lord.) Such attacks on us

for their lack of food, and I might add, our respect, sometimes causes the demonizing of the predatory animal in question, inspiring folklore or superstition, thus perhaps the reason certain animals are extinct; fear becomes our catalyst to hunt, obliterate, or drive out anything with a shady history. It is interesting that even a dolphin is a potential eater of human flesh. Remember that next time you take your kids to swim with the porpoises.

Thankfully, all things work together for the good to those who love God, and as I stated before, I believe animals naturally love God, while we are born to love the Creator. As Creator of the universe, God's redemptive qualities (I like to think) apply to all creation. The difference between the animal kingdom and us is that God gives us the choice of loving Him and the choice of rebirth. Take His hands for instance. He gathered up the dust and fashioned life from it, and if dirt to flesh isn't redemptive, I don't know what is! We see that redemptive nature in His heart to save Noah and his family and two of every species of animal on the earth. I imagine He called it all good when He was done with that too!

The Bible tells that one day there will be a new Heaven and a new Earth, and while I don't believe that God sent His only Son Jesus to save the animals, I do believe it is all part of the redemptive plan that will set the stage for the resurrection of all that is good as God intended it to be for Him and for us. The bonus will be a renewal of the animal kingdom in all of its glory, and if that means the inclusion of the purse snatcher, so be it!

Oh, and if Jesus has a dog, I don't think it is anything less than a Saint Bernard. Picture it alongside the Master going to the ends of the earth to save you! Then again, perhaps it's a Heinz 57...I have a feeling He adores mutts.

Angela

I'm leaning toward Jesus probably having a mutt; after all, He loves all of us mutts, right? And speaking of mutts...my favorite one (other than Maggie Mutt who is really a purebred with common sense) is Snoopy. Snoopy perched atop his dog house roof with his typewriter has been my source of smiles and inspiration for years and years. A thousand-piece "It was a dark and stormy night" puzzle is framed on the wall in my home sweet home office.

In 2002 I read *The Parables of Peanuts*[1] on the trip to and from our daughter Andria's law school graduation in Pennsylvania when we were living in Hawaii. What an amazing book. The content is as un-hokey as the title suggests. Grounded in solid Scripture, mingled with intelligent and relevant quotes from Bonhoeffer, Kierkegaard, Pascal, T.S. Eliot, and glittered with actual Schulz comics, there is something for every Peanuts lover, Bible scholar, and Christian thinker. Every page is thought-provoking, especially the "Jesus—The Dog God" chapter (sorry Shae). The theological insights mostly based on Isaiah 52:14 and 53:2-3 are ones not commonly presented, which makes them even more worthy of serious consideration.

Every autumn and winter season our young family watched The Great Pumpkin and Charlie Brown's Christmas. Back when we read actual newspapers, as opposed to now when we get all of our news from various Internet sources, Peanuts was the first comic I searched out. Why? *The Parables of Peanuts* answered that question. Charles Schulz said of his work, "I preach in these cartoons, and I reserve the same rights to say what I want to say as the minister in the pulpit." And preach he did. From Linus's sincere recitation of the birth of the Savior, to Charlie Brown's eternal hope of kicking the football, to Snoopy fighting the Red Baron and saving the day, and Lucy's 5-cent psychological advice, every scene evokes an emotion, thought, or memory that warms (or provokes) the soul.

For people open to allowing God to use them to spread the reality of life and His love, the world is day after day of blessings and fulfillment. Charles Schulz's life was such a life. Using the talents and skills that our heavenly Father gifted us with to make a positive difference in the lives of others is the ultimate high.

P.S. So your parrotlet has a keen appetite for manly flesh, eh, Shae? Hope that doesn't include your son's digits. I have a good friend, Sue, who has a parrotlet, Quincy, and she highly recommends the book *The Parrot Who Owns Me.* She says the book sums up her relationship with Quincy quite well, and she has no doubt that her pets will be meeting her at the Pearly Gates some day. We had a cockatiel back when wearing gold chains was in—he chewed on mine while pooping down my back. Petey moved to our nephew's house that same week.

Donna

Who can resist a mutt? My canine buddy, Rusty Boy, was pure mutt (forgive the oxymoron). If mutts were documented, his papers would have included multiple addenda to record the breeds upon breeds contributing to his DNA. He was strong as could be, healthy as an ox (there's a mutt of a metaphor for you), and had a temperament ranging from docile devotee of the family to ninja master and ruthless assassin of everyone else. The punctures in the paper boy's leather jacket were evidence to the latter. So were the mailman's halting steps up the concrete stoop leading to the assassin's front door.

Still, Jesus is an equal-opportunity lover of creation. Surely, He's just as crazy about the full-bred dachshund with the stunted legs; the ribbon-winning, curtain-eared beagle; and the spindle-legged poodle (as long as the poodle isn't sculpted with all those show-dog puffs, of course). Just *kidding*, poodle lovers! Who could resist a puffed out, pouffed up purebreed? Actually, I could. But that won't change the mind of the Maker of puffy, pouffy dogs.

Granted, if a puffy, pouffy dog adopted me in its moment of need (hard to imagine a needy show dog, but I guess it could happen), I would probably fall in a loving heap at its feet and be at the pet supply mart in a heartbeat gathering as much provision as my checkbook could handle in one day. Her big, black eyes would melt my fussy opinions and preconceived notions

about puffy, pouffy pedigrees. I have no doubt that everything in my apartment would become community property before nightfall and my penchant for sprawling diagonally across my queen-sized bed would be dismissed by dawn.

All that said, I need a little more Jesus kind of love, understanding, and wisdom where my parakeets are concerned. I adopted them when a co-worker had to return fairly suddenly and very permanently to her home state. The dead-of-winter drive would have been risky for two sensitive-to-drafts, heat-loving natives of the tropics. Not that I don't love and appreciate birds; I do (especially big birds). But Kate and Allie have been a challenge for me. They are beautiful, vocal (*very* vocal), sometimes hilarious, and perfectly crafted by God. Yet, except for the obvious fact that they are terrified of everything, they remain, at least to me, inscrutable. They are the first pets I've had that I can't figure out *at all.*

Four years in, I remain baffled. That's not their problem. It's mine. I know this much: their Creator is as in tune to them as He is to the most transparent dachshund on the planet. Matthew 6:26 tells me that. Jesus is surely the perfect parakeet lover.

Tammy

To the question of whether Jesus had a dog or not, I found this poetic answer. I offer it to you all, along with a tissue. Trust me—I needed one.

Did Christ Have a Dog?

I wonder if Christ had a dog, all curly and wooly like mine
With two silken ears and a nose round and wet, with two eyes that glisten and shine?
I'm sure if He had, the dog would have known right from the start He was God,
And needed no proof that He was divine, but just worshipped the ground that He trod.
I'm afraid that He didn't, because I have read, how He prayed in the Garden, alone,
For all His friends and disciples had fled, even Peter, the one called a "stone."
And oh, I'm sure that friendly old dog, with a heart so tender and warm,
Would never have let Him suffer alone, but creeping right under His arm
Would have licked those dear fingers in agony clasped, and counting all favors but lost,
When they led Him away would have trotted along, and died at the foot of the Cross.

—Author Unknown[2]

So maybe He didn't have a dog or a pet in the sense that we do. But I imagine that all the creatures of nature knew, and know, who He was and is. If even the wind and the waves recognized His authority, I'm certain the animal kingdom was just wiggling, fluttering, hopping, and slithering with desire to get

close to Him. However, He came to save humankind. Furry-kind had to wait.

I picture it this way: Jesus ministering to the crowds of people or talking with His disciples, all the while watched by countless adoring animal eyes, hanging back while He does His Father's work, but longing to be called to His side. And who says He wouldn't have made a little time—a moment here or there—to pet someone's ox or let a bird perch on His finger or smile at a mouse? Imagine the joy in the heart of the donkey that was chosen to carry Him into Jerusalem!

But facing the question of whether there are truly bad animals or not—my answer is bugs! Insects! Spiders! *All* of them—absolutely evil. LOL, just kidding. In spite of my personal horror of the creepy-crawlies, I can't imagine Jesus squashing out their multi-legged existences in disgust. Nope. No way. He made them too, and I'm sure He would be just as kind to them…even if my mind shudders and shies away from the image of Him petting a spider. Ugh!

Endnotes

1. Robert L. Short, *The Parables of Peanuts* (San Francisco: HarperCollins, 2002).

2. http://www.jozart3.com/dogpoems.html (accessed February 2010).

Your Reflections

Your Reflections

Your Reflections

Your Reflections

Your Reflections

Chapter 6

Common Scents

Tammy

When my Kitty is curled up on my lap, purring and smiling in his Kitty way, it's no stretch of my imagination to believe he loves me. And of course, any devoted, happy dog will inevitably look into their master's eyes with an expression that communicates such complete devotion that we humans will have no other word for it except "love."

Of course, when Kitty doesn't feel inclined to accept any lap time, I spiral into doubt—*He doesn't love me, really. Does he? Can he? Argh!* I think most of the time, what looks like love to the doting human is more like a little animal devotion, colored heavily by our biased point of view.

On the other hand, I don't want to devalue the whatever-it-is that *is* there. Because, beyond a doubt, animals can form a special connection with their humans. How many times have we heard stories of dogs that lay down and die on their master's grave? Or seen how our own emotions can trigger various responses in our pets—joy for our joy and comfort in our sorrow? What about the way my cat's behavior changes in my absence? My family has told me more than once that he gets extremely irritable and a little spastic when I'm gone for a long time. What *is* that connection between us two-shoe wearers and our four-shoe friends? (If Shae became a pooch, she'd have to double the size of her shoe closet—LOL what a thought!)

Human-style love requires a certain level of cognition and choice that I don't think animals have. Free will comes into it too—another thing creation seems to be lacking in (see Rom. 8:20). Yet creation *can* praise the Lord (see Ps. 148). I don't think that means they also praise *us*, but it does imply to me that animals are not totally mindless. I'm comforted by the thought, at least, as Kitty chooses the hearth over my lap...once again.

When it comes to the hearts of pets, maybe—in the words of my favorite band, *The Cat Empire*—"It's not exactly love, it's *to adore*." ^_^

Shae

With four legs I would not only double the size of my shoe

closet, Tammy, but also my bra drawer. I'd be a Victoria's Secret dream customer! "Uh, I'll take eight of the gels, eight of the cross-your-hearts...and do you take Visa?"

When my son was born, I saved everything—locks of hair and his um...belly button, which had fallen off the week after we brought him home. I know it sounds weird, but I just couldn't part with the umbilical cord stump, as gross-looking as it was, grasping at ways to preserve every memory, which did nothing to slow down the tick-tocks of time (he's 14 now), but did in a way help me hold on a little longer to swiftly slipping baby moments. That is, until Tango Cat ate the belly button, which by then resembled burnt bacon. No way could that fleshy morsel have appealed to him. He did it in spite, jealous of the baby. I tell you, the look on Tango's face rivaled that of Sylvester's caught with Tweety's tail feathers in his mouth. I almost pulled a Granny, wanting to whop him one with an umbrella, but instead stuck my finger down his throat to induce an upchuck. No luck. He gulped, burped, and took off. To this day I tell people that my cat carries my son's genes!

At the time, I also had a dog, my beloved Cash, a black Labrador. Don't get me started, because he died at only 8 years old of cancer, with every effort to save him. Tango always somehow managed to conscript Cash into garbage service, a weekly garbage heist involving a well-executed plan. Cat would nose open the cupboard door under the kitchen sink and claw open the hanging trash bag until the goods dropped down. Dog would drag the scraps into the living room (what *is it* with animals and carpets), where they would tear everything open and feast until

the key turned in the lock—Tango's cue to bolt and Cash's cue to hang his tail in shame. For the longest time Cash took full blame, until the day I noticed Tango peering through the banister as Cash got his "Oh you naughty puppy" scolding with, no kidding, a huge grin on his whiskered face. Cash's woeful eyes glanced from him to me as if to say, "The devil made me do it, honest!"

Cash had amazing intuitive ability. Sensing my pregnancy, he was always careful of my belly, even before I showed, and developed a hug with his forepaws gently encircling my waist and his hind legs on the floor, rather than the usual paws on the tummy. He welcomed the baby, loved on him, and fiercely protected him, and not once did he go after the milk, if you know what I mean…LOL.

One day we had an opportunity to test Cash's smarts while on a walk along the Coquitlam River. We were just passing a small sandy area when my step-daughter said, "I wonder if Cash would rescue me if he thought I was drowning?" She jumped in fully clothed, and when halfway across, treaded water, flailed her arms, splashed like crazy, and cried out, "Help! Help! Save me! Help!" Within a second Cash was in the water paddling out to her. She caught hold of his back and hung on as he faithfully pulled her to shore.

I have yet to encounter a dumb, thoughtless animal of the animal kingdom kind—few *people* would save someone's bacon. Thank You, God, for Jesus! Cash may be awaiting me in

Heaven with Jesus to celebrate my salvation. Bellybutton-eating cat, however, not so sure.

Angela

Victoria's Secret dream customer—that's you Shae! On the other hand, I've only been in that store several times, each time being tugged through the door by a daughter or two. My wallet is never the same after one of those excursions—they have no sense of common cents.

But about animals having common scents, my money's on our Maggie girl. Can I just tell you how adorable she is? (Rhetorical; I'm going to tell you anyway.) Well, it all began when we brought her home seven years ago in March. Our three older grandchildren, Anna-Lisa, Katherine, and Graye William fell in love with her at Easter time when they came for a visit. At about 10 pounds of furry fun, the kids and Maggie had a ball running from the front yard to the back yard with their baskets searching for eggs. As more grandchildren came along and Maggie steadily gained 70 more pounds, she was ever so careful around the little ones.

When daughter Samantha was expecting twins who would be only 15 months older than their "big" sister Izabella, she came to live with us while her Navy husband Kevin was in training. Maggie and Nana (that's me) became daily entertainment. Never did the little girl fear the gentle big dog. Now the

2-year-old twin tornadoes, Scarlett and Lucia, are members of the Maggie fan club too. Reasoning their vulnerability, Maggie Doodle Dog maneuvers around them gracefully…then she tries to herd them, as is her instinct. My favorite all-time comic strip that I have framed on my office wall is one of Snoopy (of course) barking and chasing each of the Peanuts gang. The last block shows all of the kids in a group and Snoopy thinking, *I would have made a good sheep dog.*

And with that, maybe I'll change my guess about Jesus having a mutt. Maybe He'd have enjoyed an Old English sheepdog like Maggie. After all, He *is* the Good Shepherd! And He knows even more than all of our vulnerabilities—and loves us anyway.

Neighbor Beverly gave me Randy Alcorn's book *Heaven*[1] while I was working on this manuscript. Her dog recently passed on, and no doubt she found comfort in the chapters devoted to animals and Heaven. One particular section caught my eye, quoting John Wesley, who spent years riding horseback to preach the Gospel. "What, if it should then please the all-wise, the all-gracious Creator to raise them [animals] higher in the scale of beings? What, if it should please Him… to make them…capable of knowing and loving and enjoying the Author of their being?"

What if, indeed.

Donna

Shae, the belly button story did me in. I'm doubled-over laughing and gagging at the same time, which seems a dangerous feat for anyone over—uh—39 who is eating a tuna sandwich. And the bra thing—well, I'd better leave it there before the side-splitting image ruptures a muscle in my midsection and commits me to a gauze and plaster corset that Victoria's Secret would disavow and the unmentionables police would be sure to mention to local fashionistas.

Seriously, I believe animals are utterly sensible, except when you turn on the vacuum, of course. Now that I mention it, Rusty Boy *was* prone to taking leave of his senses in the presence of a renegade slice of liverwurst. Truth be told, Buckwheat and Miss Crabtree did the same at the sight of olives. Nevertheless, animals whose reason is denied by members of the two-legged race are, in fact, sensible more often than not, and often more sensible than we are—even when they have ghastly plastic cones around their necks. (If you untangled that sentence, you've got better sense than I.)

We've all read maudlin stories of humans being mauled by animals. It is a fact of life. But there are also miracle stories, such as those of elephants rescuing Asian tsunami victims December 26 in 2004. Some of those stories have been disputed, but some have been checked out. Apparently, in Khao Lak, Thailand, domesticated elephants began screaming around the

time the earthquake split open the sea bed. The blessed beasts broke free of their chains and fled their low-lying terrain without a word of warning from CNN or any other human source. According to one account I read,[2] some folks assumed that the animals were aware of an unimagined, looming peril. Thankfully, some people followed the animals to higher ground and escaped the brunt force of the deadly waves. Lives were spared on the say-so of pachyderms well-packed by their Maker with good sense.

Another account bears witness to an elephant being ridden by a child as the waters receded unnaturally from the shoreline. Sensing imminent danger, the animal raced inland with its human cargo on board, saving the child's life![3] If that isn't good sense, then I don't have a clue what to call it. (BTW...have you ever read about the mourning rituals of elephants? It's mind-blowing!)

Whatever it is that animals have in the way of sense, it is *amazing.* Imagine the creatures over whom we have been given dominion saving our lives. Pretty awesome. Very God.

Endnotes

1. Randy Alcorn, *Heaven* (Carol Stream, IL: Tyndale House Publishers, Inc.), 403.

2. "Elephantasy," snopes.com, http://www.snopes.com/critters/defender/elephant.asp (accessed March 5, 2010).

3. Ibid.

Your Reflections

Your Reflections

Your Reflections

Your Reflections

Your Reflections

Chapter 7

Lassie Left Behind?

Angela

If "the rapture" happened tomorrow, do I think the animals would be included? Yes! Can you imagine Heaven without the pitter patter of puppy paws or the purring of a preening kitty? In Heaven would the glistening blue pond waters be without elegant white swans gracefully gliding across? Would the shore be missing waddling momma ducks and fluffy little yellow ones trying to keep up? No. In fact, I can't wait to see all of the animals that I haven't had the pleasure of seeing while on earth, like a snow leopard and koala bear (missed seeing them at the really awesome San Diego Zoo) and the newly discovered adorable scale-crested pygmy tyrant (Google it—too cute!). To see bunnies hopping beside wolves and

lions and lambs sleeping peacefully near each other will be sweet indeed.

No longer will Maggie instinctively bark at the deer and squirrels who live in the woods behind our home or chase the cats that stray into our yards. I look forward to the day when the nervous little house wren won't flitter away quickly when I water the flowers in the window box where she chose to hatch her little speckled brown eggs. How fun it will be to have a close-up look at the hummingbirds who enjoy my garden's coral bells each summer. But will I warm up to snakes? I don't think so.

I might be all wet about what Heaven will actually be like, but I'm looking forward to swimming in a clear blue ocean without fearing the da-dum da-dum da-dum music from *Jaws* overshadowing the pleasure of the refreshing saltwater gently swaying me with the tide. And how about taking walks in the mountains without worrying about stepping on something of the rattle type or having to run from something not of the friendly Winnie the Pooh type? I think God will (or certainly does now) enjoy having all of His creation mingling down His streets of gold, His emerald fields, mountains of silver, and sapphire waters under ruby-streaked skies with pearlescent clouds.

I wax poetic to give my mind a breath of life and color as outside my office windows today is served only gray-brown leftovers of winter cold. What a few weeks ago was covered with an 18-inch thick blanket of beautiful pure white snow, now reveals

sickly looking grass, leafless trees, empty flower pots, stubby bare bushes, and naked patios and decks.

"Looking forward" is hope in the future. As I look forward to spring bringing life back to outdoor nature, as I look forward to welcoming two new "baby grands" into the world this year, as I look forward to completing my memoir, as I look forward to my ultimate reward—Heaven—I have the assurance that I will enjoy the fellowship of Jesus, my dear departed parents, friends, and relatives...and I won't be surprised if I see Lassie, Rin Tin Tin, Flipper, and That Darn Cat!

Donna

As much as I love animals, I'd be lying if I said that their eternal disposition was high on my list of concerns. Like I've said before, I don't think animals worry about it at all. More than that, it's where people spend eternity that weighs on my mind. Those are the kinds of consequences that get my knickers in a bunch. That may sound unfeeling to some animal lovers; I certainly don't mean it to be, and I'm sorry if it seems harsh. I just think it cuts to the heart of the matter—the Bible says God created *us* in His image. How can I argue with Him on that or add to it? I can't. The Scriptures don't say anything about my beloved Skippy, Rusty Boy, Cherry Baby, Buckwheat, Miss Crabtree, Kate, or Allie being created in anybody's image or being redeemed by the blood of the Savior. Far as I can tell, whatever God chooses for them is out of my hands.

Our God is Triune: Father, Son, and Holy Spirit. We are triune beings, too, having spirit, soul, and body. I guess, depending upon your stream of Christianity, definitions vary. In my spiritual neck of the woods, I go with the concept of *soul* as comprising the mind, will, and emotions. I have no doubt in my mind that Rover possesses all three. He can think through situations (he certainly knows where to find a good Jimmy Choo-bone, no matter what you do to hide it). He's smart enough to mutilate the costly shoe while his mistress is at work. For sure, he has a will: how many times has he had his snout stung over a shoe shredding and he *still* comes back for more? And bless his heart, Rover has emotions. After mauling that Choo Perfect Peep Toe and getting a good dose of what-for, doesn't Rover's hang-dog countenance just tear you up? You know the look: the darting brow and drooping eyes (did I see a tear beginning to form?), the dog jaw dragging along the floor amid nappa shreds of evidence that remind him of his short-lived victory, the grunt of resignation and self-pity...you get the idea.

But Rover having a spirit? I don't think so. That doesn't mean God can't use an animal if He wants to. He certainly used an ass quite nicely (see Num. 22). Nor do I think the absence of a spirit precludes the presence of animals in Heaven. I think Heaven will be the most "complete" place we have ever known. We know it will contain mansions and streets of gold and none of those things have spirits. I reckon God can put whatever He wants in Heaven. And whatever that is, it will be *phenomenal.*

Tammy

Do animals have spirits? My dear old college buddy pointed me to this King James gem: *"Who knoweth the spirit of man that goeth upward, and the spirit of the beast that goeth downward to the earth?"* (Eccles. 3:21 KJV). I read that and got a little wide-eyed and slack-jawed…then clamped my jaw shut and silently decided I didn't like the King James anymore. King Jimmy and I are friends no longer. (LOL, kidding!) ^_^

I *did* have to hurry off to my personal favorite version, though, just for a little affirmation and help. Here it is in context:

> *For that which befalls the sons of men befalls beasts; even [in the end] one thing befalls them both. As the one dies, so dies the other. Yes, they all have one breath and spirit, so that a man has no preeminence over a beast; for all is vanity (emptiness, falsity, and futility)! All go to one place; all are of the dust, and all turn to dust again. Who knows the spirit of man, whether it goes upward, and the spirit of the beast, whether it goes downward to the earth?* (Ecclesiastes 3:19-21 AMP)

Whew, OK! More of an "if" thing. I can deal! Especially since this passage is from the precious old Book of Ecclesiastes.

Does *"Everything is meaningless!"* ring a bell? (See Ecclesiastes 1:2 NIV.) Now, don't misunderstand me—the Old Testament is just as much God's relevant, inspired Word as the New. But this writer also had not yet seen the glorious work of Christ on the Cross. (I think such a revelation would have been just the dose of joy this poor guy needed.) We who look back on that moment of infinite love and grace are able to say with joyful assurance, "Yes, I *know* my spirit is going upward! I'm already riding the celestial escalator, baby! Praise the Lord, my destination is way, way *up!*"

Thing is, the New Testament doesn't really add any revelation that would assure us that animals have upward-bound spirits too—nothing more than an eventual "liberation" for creation, which Paul alludes to (see Rom. 8:21). In the absence of biblical say-so, I guess it's up to each of us to just trust the Lord and rely on His goodness and wisdom. And really, if you have to seek an answer to the eternal destination of the household bundle of fluffy joy, just ask Him. I'll be praying that He gives each questioning reader an answer, but more than that—peace.

Me? I asked, and He *didn't* answer with a yes or a no. But He *did* offer His perfect peace. So I trust He'll work everything for the best, and I will one day (hopefully not too soon!) entrust my beloved Kitty into His loving hands.

"Who knows...if the spirit of the animal goes down into the earth?" (Eccles. 3:21 NIV). God knows. And He's awesome. Me? I've no idea. ^_^

Shae

All is not lost! Solomon certainly indicates animals as having some sort of spirit (see also Eccles. 12:7). Ours was made for God, designed for the heavenly, higher world, and perhaps the soul of an animal was created to derive its happiness from this lower world. Moreover, perhaps animals will have a resurrection to have endless enjoyment not in Heaven, but in the new earth with us! Remember, Heaven is only for a little while; we will be living forever on a new earth.

For sure our rightness with God is of utmost importance. This is why I do not chain myself to trees in the name of saving spotted owls; there are yet too many human souls that need saving. But I also believe that in our securing of the animal kingdom's well-being and in our stewardship of the environment, we *fulfill* the creative joy and purpose of God. We see God's concern for ours and the animals' welfare, particularly when He extended mercy to the city of Nineveh, not only for the 120,000 innocent children there, but also for the "many animals" (see Jon. 4:11). It doesn't surprise me, since animals were, as you quoted, created in much the same ashes-to-ashes and dust-to-dust way we were formed.

God thought enough of His animals to give Adam the opportunity of providing each species a name. You don't name something you don't deeply care about. Wow, it blows me away to think about God's creative genius—His awesome mind

whirring as He fashioned fish, birds, and wildlife, their shapes and instincts. What *was* He thinking with the platypus…it's as if He decided to play a joke on Adam. *Well, let Me just see what My boy will call THIS one!* I imagine Adam had a jaw-dropping time of it naming the animals. I mean, have you checked out the blob fish or the frill-necked lizard, and man, those kangaroo pockets—every shoe shopper should have one (not to mention a roo's bounce!).

As far as I can see, throughout the Bible animals (evil serpent aside) are already in right relationship with God, have never degenerated in rebellion as we have, and do not need forgiveness and salvation as we do. This should humble us, as we remember that God has fixed a day when He will judge the whole world with justice, while we also remember the words of Proverbs 12:10, *"A good man takes care of his animals, but wicked men are cruel to theirs"* (paraphrased). Scripture is clear concerning creation and our responsibility to treat animals with love and care; we will one day give account of our conduct to the Creator. Which reminds me of the time, as kids, when we sent toads to their death by racing them down rocks on their bellies, skinning them alive. Forgive Me, Father, for I have sinned; how horrible!

It is only humankind who needs forgiving and saving and teaching in the ways of worship, for the animal kingdom worships God continually and naturally (see Ps. 36; 51), as I stated before. It is, to quote Donna, "very God" to reveal that all of His creation has contact with Him (see Ps. 93), that all His creatures praise Him (see Ps. 145:10). This would indicate to

me that an animal does indeed have some sort of spirit, though different from ours, one in continual adoration. Scripture is clear. A time will come in the final climax of the ages when *all creation* faces the Creator: the four living creatures around the Throne, the twenty-four elders, the redeemed, the angels, and all living beings *present* their worship to Almighty God (see Rev. 4:5-6;12). The ultimate "Godstock" filled with God huggers. Won't that rock?

Your Reflections

Your Reflections

Your Reflections

Your Reflections

Your Reflections

Chapter 8

Scratching at St. Peter's Door

Shae

As much as I would like to think that Gracie has the same ticket to Heaven that the Bible tells me I have, I know in my heart she is not anywhere near as concerned because her unregenerated dog spirit is limited to the things of dogs, in the same way the unregenerated human spirit is limited to the things of man, with no ability to appreciate salvation, no more than a hog would appreciate a genuine pearl necklace (see Matt. 7:6). As Donna eluded, it is important that we understand our tripartite nature to even begin to understand our differences.

In his book, *Rightly Dividing the Word,* Dr. Clarence Larkin uses three concentric circles to illustrate our threefold nature.

The outer circle stands for the body of humankind, the middle circle for the soul, and the inner circle for the spirit. He states that the outer circle touches the material world through the five senses of sight, smell, hearing, taste, and touch. The middle circle represents the soul, which is the imagination, conscience, reason, memory, and affections (commonly known as the seat of our affections), and acts as a gateway to the flesh or gateway into the inner circle of the spirit, the spirit being our sphere of God-consciousness and encompassing our faculties of faith, hope, reverence, prayer, and worship. It is also a place where we are enabled to investigate, think, weigh evidence, and surrender our will, and it is where we are divinely renewed, regenerated, AKA born again. The one thing that stands guard at the door of our spirits is our own will, that of the soul, which is where satan operates, making his appeal to our affections and emotions, feeding us lies.

Once the will is surrendered to God, however, the Holy Spirit comes to live in the human spirit, the Spirit Himself (the Holy Spirit) bearing witness with our spirits, the truth that we are children of God (see Rom. 8:16). Our spirits, which essentially are our personalities, hidden in Christ, differentiate us from the animal creation, in that we are able to worship Him in spirit *and* in *truth*, gradually growing in truth to become more like Jesus. The inspiration of the Almighty, Spirit to spirit, gives us understanding (see Job 32:8). Animals would not have the Holy Spirit living within, providing them any such witness, guarantee, or regeneration. They simply exist in their respective spirits, which I do think can be possessed, as in the demons Jesus cast out of the demoniac and into the swine, or controlled

by God for His earthly purposes. They would not, therefore, have a heavenly desire or hope.

Nor would the human spirit without the spiritual spark of regeneration direct its affections and desires toward the truth; the human spirit can never appreciate the Cross unless born from above, unless realizing its sinful condition and understanding God's grace in salvation.

For now, Gracie is just content to be the gift to me that she is, and I am content with Christ being the gift to me that He is; and I look far more forward to seeing Him than I do any of my dearly departed animals in Heaven. One glimpse of my beautiful Savior is all I need! It is more than enough! And if He just happens to be walking my dearly departed beloved Cash when He greets me in Heaven, precious bonus!

Angela

Wow, Shae, you must have had on your "very sensible" shoes and your French manicure must have chipped away while writing your deep and inspirational comments for this "scratching at the door" chapter. I thought I was back in Comparative World Religion class at the university! For sure the intricacies of the spirit, soul, and body are fascinating, and I agree that animals don't share our privilege of the Holy Spirit's indwelling. That said, God is more than capable, if He so desires, of providing them their own special connection to Him…and Heaven.

After all, His thoughts and ways are not anywhere close to ours (see Isa. 55:8).

The arrogance of "man" (as in "all people") is evident from the beginning when satan puffed up Adam and Eve's chests with the too-tempting "you'll be like God" ploy. Most of the Old Testament is about people who failed to depend on and trust totally in God. Rather, they thought they could live better feeding off their own egos. Much of the New Testament is about how Jesus came to save us from ourselves. In that light, He is our Savior, our Redeemer, our sacrificial Lamb.

Thousands of animals and birds were sacrificed to God before He offered the ultimate One. The proxies must have been meaningful to God the Father, and no doubt He wept knowing that they were insufficient to cleanse the dirt and grime humankind loved (and continues to love) to grovel in. Each sacrifice was and is meaningful. The sacrifice of Jesus Christ changed humankind's relationship with the Great I Am for eternity. Because God so loved the world, He gave His only begotten Son, that whosoever believes in Him will not perish, but will have everlasting life! (See John 3:16.) Hallelujah!

As part of that eternal life, I am quite sure that much of what our finite minds have "discovered" and "studied" and "thought about" will seem silly. Daily we will be amazed at all the loftier things, people, places, and yes, animals, that He created for His pleasure. We and all living creatures and beasts will be singing "Holy, holy, holy, Lord God Almighty, who was, and is, and is to come," because He is worthy to receive glory and honor and

power; for He has created all things and for His pleasure they are and were created (see Rev. 4:8,11).

Tammy

Heaven—populated by as many Christian pets as redeemed human beings, if not more? Well, let's hope the perfecting of creation takes care of creation's mess-making habits! (See Romans 8:19-21.) Otherwise, get ready for some paw prints tracking mud on the streets of gold! Not to mention some serious shedding all over the mansions He has prepared for us. (But then, would it really be a mansion *for me* without my Kitty's fur all over the place?) ^_^ I trust, of course, that when the Lord wipes every tear from our eyes, that will include eye-watering allergic reactions to the pet next door.

Yeah, heavenly pet ownership would have to be a different story from the earthly variety, wouldn't it? After all, isn't He making all things new? (See Revelation 21:5 NASB.) I guess that means no allergies, no clawing up the heavenly furniture, no messing on the golden rugs, and no tracking celestial dirt all over the place. (Though I'm making an assumption here—the Bible doesn't promise freedom from housecleaning in Heaven, but come on. I think we can safely hope for that one.) The beloved fluff-balls will surely have left their shoe-chewing days behind them, Shae! Will we even wear shoes in Heaven? Or, perhaps a better question—will we notice whether or not we're wearing them, once faced with Jesus' glory and love?

In fact, if our pets join us in Heaven, will they even be *our* pets anymore? Sure, God gave us dominion over all creation, but isn't it all His? We might find that in Heaven all our beloved pets, once entrusted to our care, are now joyfully adoring our Lord alongside us. And He can receive worship and love from His Bride *and* His pets! It's just a far-fetched guess from a girl who chases thoughts like a puppy goes after sticks, but it paints a pretty heavenly and glorious picture in my mind! Forget just being free of pain or sickness—an eternity of meowing, barking, squawking, and singing His praise is a *real* Heaven experience. ^_^

Donna

Since I don't have—forgive me!—a dog in this hunt, I'll let my imagination run hog-wild. (Thankfully, I don't have any hogs in the hunt either, although I hear they are quite lovable, in a sloppy kind of way.) Speaking of sloppy—if the divine plan includes heavenly hospitality for the critters I have loved, I'm thinking my parakeets' cage and its upkeep will be history. Hallelujah! And if my beloved Buckwheat and Miss Crabtree are in Heaven, they will be litter box-less, right? I will have scooped up my last pebble-encased delicacy, forever!

Maybe my buddy Rusty will be stretched out in a suave pose on the cool streets of gold. He'll be best friends with the paper boy he tried to maul every Friday (the day the poor kid had to walk up to the door to collect the cash-ola), and he

will have made eternal amends with the mailman he terrorized for 18 years, assuming the mailman made it through the Gate (there's a sobering thought). My dad's brand-new suede jacket (the one Rusty tore to shreds while we were at work and school) will be a non-issue. The offense that almost got the pup transferred out of Scuderi Land would never impact his standing in Heaven if entry were granted to man's best friend.

A Heaven-bound Skippy will be squeaky clean all the time and probably surrounded by angels, so there's no chance a 2-year-old will dunk him in the john. Which raises the whole issue of hygiene and plumbing in Heaven. Anyway, Skippy would be a new man and I, his unwitting tormentor, would not cause the fur on his back to rise.

As for my six-and-seven-toed kitty, Cherry Baby—she will have long forgotten her territorial wars with Rusty Boy and presumably, her bouts with Mikey, the killer cat that joined the Scuderi family after I'd left the roost. (The less said about Mikey, the better.) As for Paul and Ringo, our turtles, Ringo won't be climbing out of his turtle house and falling over the edge of the fridge into the swing-top trash pail full of kitchen refuse anymore. Ringo was quite the aerialist in his day and perhaps more of a scavenger than we realized.

Should Jesus come before my dachshund does, maybe one will be waiting for me in Heaven. That would be sweet! Maybe he'll look just like Frank, my neighbor's amazingly wonderful adult doxie. Frank is the perfect reddish-brown shorthair. He has the disposition of a saint and puts up with his master's new

addition—a hyperactive, attention-consuming longhair who was recently weaned. He (or she??) is adorable, but a handful. Anyway, maybe I'll have a weiner-dog named Frank.

Frank or no Frank, Heaven will be perfect. I only wish every person would choose to call it home.

Your Reflections

Your Reflections

Your Reflections

Your Reflections

Your Reflections

Chapter 9

Reveille for Rover

Shae

Your cat has seven toes, Donna? Did the other paw at one time have seven, before Rusty? And let me tell you about hogs. They are *not* cute. I live about a mile away (as the crow flies) from the Robert Pickton pig farm. Pickton, a serial killer (convicted of murdering six women, charged in the deaths of an additional 20, but suspected of at least 50 killings), fed his victims to the pigs, which of course went to market. I've been off pork since 2002! It is hard to say good-bye to our pets, but can you imagine the grief of the parents and families of those missing women? It does put things in perspective.

The Lord knows we spent so much money trying to save Cash, heal him of his cancer. But the farewell was sweet. Cash somehow mustered energy to eat a rice meatball, his favorite food, and I remember thinking, *how can he be so sick and yet eat?* I'm convinced he did it more to appease me than anything else. Then, he put his head in my lap and his chocolate eyes looked up as though to say, "It's OK. I'm ready." My son and the vet joined us on the floor, and with the three of us laying beside him, holding and petting him, giving him soft words of encouragement, the vet administered the lethal injection, and Cash just settled into his final sleep with a deep sigh. Oh my goodness, I'm crying as I write this, recalling my young son's tears—he'd always known Cash—and even the vet's weeping as the champ, this nonjudgmental furry love source, took his last breath. We scattered Cash's ashes (great book title!) by the river.

My sister only recently removed the ash remains of three of her departed pets from a shrine she had created in her living room. I can well understand why she enshrined them so, in the absence of having children, which she so earnestly desired. Today, she and her husband have a new baby they call Tiki Barber, a Chihuahua rescue, and they are happier than I've seen in decades! In a way, Tiki has even helped improve their marriage, much more laughter!

I don't think it bothers God that we love our animals so. He Himself is so tenderhearted and loves all creatures great and small. I am sure it touches His heart when we do suffer such losses that He does not consider our cries over our lost pets

wasted tears. In fact, it would not surprise me one bit if His plan all along, in allowing us to make pets of His animals, was for the very purpose of creating in our hearts the question of eternity, which ultimately directs hearts toward Him. All along His plan may have been to use them to put us in touch with our Creator, to restore the wonder of His love and His very hope for us. The question, "Will my pet go to Heaven?" swings open a door that can lead to the incredible spiritual truth: the awesome conviction of "God sees the little sparrow fall, He meets its tender view, if God so loves the little birds, I know He loves me too." Amen, He loves you too!

Angela

Not long ago I emailed my good friend Sharon about being at the vet clinic with Maggie for a checkup and watching a big, football player-type teenager emerge from a room crying like a baby and hearing a woman sobbing, "I'm sorry, I'm so sorry, I'm sorry..." It was obvious what happened. I cried too—then and now. My friend's return email included the following compassionate sentiment that she received when faced with this very hard decision:

You're giving me a special gift,
So sorrowfully endowed,
And through these last few cherished days,
Your courage makes me proud.

But really, love is knowing
When your best friend is in pain,
And understanding earthly acts
Will only be in vain.

So looking deep into your eyes,
Beyond, into your soul,
I see in you the magic, that will
Once more make me whole.

The strength that you possess,
Is why I look to you today,
To do this thing that must be done,
For it's the only way.

That strength is why I've followed you,
And chose you as my friend,
And why I've loved you all these years…
My partner 'til the end.

Please, understand just what this gift,
You're giving, means to me,
It gives me back the strength I've lost,
And all my dignity.

You take a stand on my behalf,
For that is what friends do.
And know that what you do is right,
For I believe it too.

So one last time, I breathe your scent,
And through your hand I feel,
The courage that's within you,
To now grant me this appeal.

Cut the leash that holds me here,
Dear friend, and let me run,
Once more a strong and steady cat,
My pain and struggle done.

And don't despair my passing,
For I won't be far away,
Forever here, within your heart,
And memory I'll stay.

I'll be there watching over you,
Your ever faithful friend,
And in your memories I'll run,
...a lively kitten once again.

Donna

Life is real. As I super-size the tissues, I tackle the memories of how hard it is to say good-bye to our beloved pets. And the difficult decision to euthanize, well, it just seems to make things harder, IMHO. You find yourself naming the day and hour in which you and your devoted friend must part. It adds to the burden of separation. That load lingers in the heart, even

as the grief of the actual separation abates. As I pictured Cash's final moments, Shae, my mind wandered back to my good-byes to Buckwheat and Miss Crabtree. It was as though, one day, they were fabulous 15-year-olds who would live forever, and suddenly, both of them were gravely ill.

Several weeks had passed since my two buddies began "having accidents." Other than Buckwheat's early childhood assault on the 12-button sofa, there had been no challenges with feline toileting, so to speak. "The goils," as I called them in affectionate Brooklynese, were immaculate in their habits. Still, my work schedule had edged off the charts. Life had become chaotic in many ways, as I recall. I reasoned that the goils were not as tolerant of upheaval as they had been in their younger years. You know how vocal goils can be. I suspected they were giving me what for and punctuating it in ways I could not ignore. So I doted over them when I was home and patiently spent nights and mornings on carpet rehab.

Then Miss Crabtree began vomiting and my run as a cat psychologist came to an abrupt end. Something was *wrong*. Next thing I knew, the vet and I had a crushing heart-to-heart. I could delay the end, but the end was coming, and soon—for both of my goils. On a spring evening, we gathered in the kitchen for our final farewells. Shae, I can still feel the sigh that followed each injection. I held them, one at a time, and felt each of my beautiful friends give up the ghost. I cried and cried and cried. I still weep every time I think about it. It's not that I equate the deaths of my pets with the deaths of the people I love. I don't. It's not even close. Yet, somehow, those two feisty

critters owned a piece of my heart, and their untimely end seemed to seal off that piece forever.

Will I see them again? I don't know. I *can* bank on this one thing: we had 15 amazing years together. They had a wonderful life and added so much joy to mine.

Three cheers for the goils—and forever thanks to the Father who loaned them to me. I will always remember the blessing.

Tammy

I'm with you guys on this topic—it's a tear-jerker! I even start thinking about saying good-bye, and my nose goes redder than a red-nosed reindeer's and starts sniffling worse than any hay fever effect. My excuse—a good one I might add—is that my darling Kitty, the most comforting animal I ever loved, who has been through thick and thin with me, is getting well up there in years, has been slowing down considerably, and has begun to see the occasional health problem, too. I tell you, I can't let my mind travel far into the future on the subject of Kitty or any of his fuzzy, four-legged kin. I know the day is coming for him, but to be honest, I can't deal with imagining it.

I wasn't there when the vet paid us a last visit and my family bid farewell to our dear chow-lab-retriever mutt, Dolly. In another state at college at the time, I had to say my good-byes a

few months in advance, knowing her days were numbered. But the parting moment—I wasn't there for that.

My first two cats, both outdoor-only, ended their days while I was still a child. Neither one was ever found—they both just went off, as animals sometimes do when they know it's their time, and didn't provide an opportunity for good-byes. As hard as it would have been, especially at my age at the time, I think I would have wished for the chance to say good-bye. Instead of that sharp, final pain, I had to struggle for some time with the uncertainty and doubt that comes with no-proof territory. I've since handed Jerry and Sowie over to Jesus' care, but it took awhile to get there, I'll admit.

Of course, our family has also had numerous fish and rodents. The fish I won't mention—my theory is that it's hard to fall in love with an animal you never touched, at least for me. The guinea pigs were my sister's, but it was tragic to lose them. The gerbils were mine, and as much as the little critters were totally brainless—I swear—I still mourned their loss. Frisky, Risky, Pinky, and Candy all passed away in my arms… er, hands. Yes, it was miserably sad, even though they were only rodents. But truly, I have no regrets with those little scurriers. I think it's because I was there to see them off.

It's no fun at all to face that final parting, and it can shred the heart to make the decision to name the time and place, but I wouldn't trade the chance. I've had enough experiences with losing pets and not being able to be there with them. Even if

Kitty's farewell is beyond my ability to picture, I hope I'm there for it.

Pass those super-sized tissues, please, Donna.

Your Reflections

Your Reflections

Your Reflections

Your Reflections

Your Reflections

Chapter 10

Our Personal Pet Stories

Angela

Maggie's Tale

As an Old English sheepdog, the Mrs. and Mr. Man thought a good name for me would be Margaret Thatcher. I agreed, and looked forward to fulfilling my role as the prime mistress of the house. Winston Churchill would also have worked, as they had me "fixed" right away, something about "already too many unwanted dogs in the world, blah, blah, blah."

I quickly taught them to let me outside when I needed to do my business and that I needed a treat upon return from

my stroll around the yard sending terror through squirrels and cats alike. Before long, I made it known that I also liked an occasional dollop of ice cream and I *love* white American cheese. Being spoiled is the only way to live!

They had just returned from living in Hawaii for three years, and I suppose their house and hearts seemed too big and empty, so they filled them up with me. Oh happy day! Their only expectations in return for providing all my needs and wants: greet them at the door wagging my stubby tail, catch the toy when tossed in the air, sit when spoken to, and sleep more on the Mrs.'s side of the bed in the wintertime to keep her feet warm.

Always the workaholics, twice-retired Mr. Man (remember that lady running out the front door calling "Mr. Man, Mr. Man" in Blues Brothers? I love that movie.) opened a boutique custom framing store (AKA small hometown business) and I became his mascot—even had my picture in the local weekly newspaper! All the customers love me. When I'm not lounging at the store like a big, cuddly Gund stuffed toy, I'm with the Mrs. in her home office lying beside her pink-slippered feet, especially if she's snacking on cream puffs, nachos, or cookies. One flip of my long eyelashes over my big hungry-look eyes is good for one bite for every bite she takes. This system works out well as I weigh about 80 pounds and she's about 30 pounds heavier—sharing with me makes her feel not as junk-food guilty.

I love kids. Sometimes the "grands" come to visit from Florida and Virginia and we have a blast. I get more treats than

Lassie had episodes! When there's a bunch of them, I like to try and herd them around the back yard. They don't really get it, but then again, neither did the sheep in that *Babe* movie.

Not long ago, Mr. Man and the Mrs. took me to the vet because I was limping. Turns out I have arthritis; Ms. Doc said it was typical now that I'm a "senior." Geez louise a senior at 7—that's harsh. Now I know why the Mrs. moaned when she started getting senior citizen stuff in the mail when she recently turned 55. It's not fun getting "more mature."

I don't know if I'll go to Heaven or not. But I do know that I've had a good life—better than a lot of pets. And I know I've brought a lot of smiles to a lot of people. If that's the sum total of my existence, then that's OK with me.

Donna

Sweet Maggie, I wish Buckwheat could share the tale of a long-ago, dismal night in New York City. Freezing rain drove most people off the streets. Bitter temperatures, slick surfaces, and the stinging assault of frozen needles from the sky transformed every sofa in five boroughs into the finest suite on earth.

I no longer remember what activity consumed the daylight hours, but it involved considerable traffic in and out of my apartment. I remember watching to prevent the cats from

escaping. At some point, the watching was over and I settled in for a quiet night with the "goils," who typically stuck close by me, or at least checked in with a nose-bump every now and then.

Miss Crabtree followed the usual formula. Buckwheat didn't. Soon, Buckwheat's uninterrupted absence raised a red flag. I called her name repeatedly. No response. I shook the box of dry food. Nothing. I opened the cabinet where cans of wet food were stored. Nada. My heart rate accelerated. The apartment was tiny enough that I could search it in a matter of seconds, which I did—behind the etageres...under the coach...in the bathtub...in the small space on the far side of the large platform bed that was wedged into my tiny bedroom. No Buckwheat. My mouth was parched as I looked in the last possible hiding place—the large storage drawer under the bed. Neither cat had ever found a way into the space, and I was fairly neurotic about preventing their becoming trapped there inadvertently. I hadn't used the drawer that day; but checking it was my only hope. If not there, then she was on the mean streets in the freezing rain.

I called her name as I rummaged through the drawer's contents. No Buckwheat and no sound. My worst fears were upon me: Buckwheat was somewhere *out there.*

I suited up and searched the streets for I don't know how long. After awhile, I summoned other searchers (my brother, I think, and a boyfriend answered the call). It was a needle-in-a-haystack scenario and, with the limited visibility, hope was not exactly burning brightly. Buckwheat was nowhere to be found.

I remember returning to my apartment brokenhearted. Crabby looked at me with head tilted and eyes pleading. "I'm going to put on some dry clothes, girl. I'm going back out there to find 'Wheatie."

In disbelief that she could be gone, I searched the apartment one last time. Hoping against hope, I slid out the underbed storage drawer one more time. No meows, no nothing. Then—hallelujah!—it happened! A wiry tail emerged from the blankets. Immediately, the boulder pressing against my chest lifted. Questions as to *how* and *why* evaporated as I snatched up my wayward pal and squished her against me, slobbering tears and kisses all over her tiny frame.

The relationship between humans and beasts is heavenly!

Tammy

In a fine town down South, my childhood home,
Was a neighborhood filled with cats who would roam
Free as the birds, with no one to care.
I met my fated new fuzzy friend there.

One day down my street he strutted his stuff,
That teeny-tiny, orange, soft ball of fluff,
And into my hands he was thenceforth committed:
A stray kitten and kid most perfectly fitted.

For months we waited, suspended in fear,
Hoping the answer we'd finally hear
Would be, "OK, keep him." Yet long so was our wait
By the time that answer at last sealed our fate,

He'd been going by "kitty" entirely too long.
The association had just grown too strong!
So Kitty he stayed, and Kitty was named,
And at first I thought, "Well, ***she*** *won't be ashamed."*

Until the vet fixed our horrible slip
When we took "her" in for a little "snip-snip."
We learned that ***he*** *needed a different procedure…*
But the name still stuck, whether for "him" or "her."

So Kitty became my own darling kitten,
Took over the household and really fit in.
He met a small challenge to his supreme reign
In the form of a hyper Lab puppy's disdain.

But Kitty, who'd been a street cat so tough,
Soon taught that pup that enough was enough.
Friends they became, year in and year out,
Both part of the family, there was no doubt.

Northward we moved, bringing those two,
Though the car trip was a miserable trial to go through.
(At least for the cat, the dog didn't care.)
And now Kitty had a new home to share.

A neighborhood tamer, fewer felines to fight,
Though his mommy still makes him come in for the night.
A fireplace obviously made just for him,
And birds and rabbits for his predator whim,

A lap always loving and warm for his naps,
A family of real sensible, cat-loving chaps.
The perfect arrangement for him, all in all,
From winter to spring to summer to fall.

As he reaches his upper years, now slowing down,
The family still admits that he wears the crown,
A regal old gent, silent and clever,
And orange and—truth be told—fluffy as ever.

The dog's gone on ahead, the cat still sticks around,
Planning on 20 more years, I'll be bound!
But whether his years will be many or few
I'll never find a companion so faithful and true.

Through laughter and sunshine or tears and cold snow,
His life has blessed mine like he'll never know.

Shae

I'm all storied out, so consider this a pet "peeve" story! Hey, only sisters will read this right? Please lock this in your vault.

I "menopawsed" early, before I was 40. I was in that 1 percent category of younger women who suffer through it. As a result, imagine my shock when, while yet a babe, I discovered my first whisker. A friend pointed it out at a wedding. She tried to pluck the brawny bristle off of me, but it uncoiled and strangled her. Bless her heart and may she rest in peace.

I had handled everything else—the mood disturbances, phantom pains, dry skin—with below-average decorum, but I needed cognitive therapy for the paintbrush growing on my chin. I could paint the Sistine Chapel with it (or sweep the patio). Combined with hot flashes, it was a recipe for prickly heat I tell you!

Whiskers don't exactly fit my image of femininity or enhance my female prowess. My son concurs and tells me I'm metamorphosing into a man. In retort one morning, I explained that someday his body too would change and he'd grow boobs. But he didn't buy it. "Hey mom, in a year or two, you can give me shaving lessons."

"Why don't you run off and play with that bully next door like a good boy," I barked. He high-tailed it out of there, only narrowly dodging a flying tweezer.

It's time I go on a quest to find out why I'm beginning to look like my wiry terrier, Gracie, because things are getting serious. The other day in the park, a Great Dane mistook me for her. It will take forever to get the yellow stain off my beautiful white jeans.

Perhaps animal science will give me a clue. Until then, every day I pluck, pluck, pluck. But my girlfriends tell me not to.

"Give me one good reason," I say.

They'll grow back a hundred-fold, wirier, coarser…

Hello? I am all woman. Whiskers conflict with my feminine nature (which begs the question: Did Eve shave?).

They give you character…

What, the character of a porcupine?

It's the way God made you…

As in gorilla?

Look, despite what you might be thinking, I'm not obsessed with my looks. I just don't want to be mistaken for a nanny goat, OK?

Sigh, if things continue the way they are, Gracie will be the one asking God, "Will my pet go to Heaven?"

I sure hope God says, "Yes!"

Your Reflections

Your Reflections

Your Reflections

Your Reflections

Your Reflections

Conclusion

So will your pet go to Heaven? Only God knows for sure; but we hope our banter and chatter gave you some "paws" for thought, tickled your feathered fancy, and maybe stirred some favorite furry fond memories.

Life is all about relationships, love, and death—with a lot of other "stuff" in-between. Does the other stuff really count? Well, if you believe in a heavenly Father who loves us more desperately than anyone could ever love a pet, then yes. It does count. It counts how we react to that grumpy neighbor, the teacher who picks on your best friend, the spouse who continues to load the dishwasher the "wrong way."

It counts that we have hope—hope in the people and events past that have made us better, not bitter. Hope in the current

days of blessings and the glasses that are half full, not empty. Hope in the future minutes, hours, days, months, and years to be filled with God working in our lives to bring about His perfect plan for us, our beloved families and friends, and treasured pets.

It counts that we share the good news of how Jesus died for our sins and lives today to bring all of His children into life abundant now and sweet bliss eternal later. It counts that we are good public relations people for the Creator, the Prince of Peace and our Redeemer. Life counts.

From Maggie to Kitty to Gracie and Wally to Kate and Allie and all of the Rovers and Tweeties between, I thank God for the way they complete and bring comfort in life for many people. Almighty God knew that even the best of people-to-people relationships are sometimes too full of "blah, blah, blah," and not enough silent tail wagging, purring, and melodic warbling. Those of us too self-conscious (or fill in any word that fits) to talk aloud our innermost feelings and thoughts to another person can easily confide in a pet who won't judge us or our motives—or our sanity.

We completed writing this book on Palm Sunday, with the emotional roller coaster ride through Maundy Thursday, Good Friday, and Easter approaching. Thinking about Holy Week and Heaven brings to mind one of my most favorite and comforting Scripture passages. The man hanging on his cross beside Jesus on His cross said, *"'Lord, remember me when You come into Your kingdom.' And Jesus said to him, 'Assuredly, I say to*

you, today you will be with Me in Paradise'" (Luke 23:42-43). All who believe are assured a place with Him in Heaven.

As pets come and go, we know there is only One who will never leave us or forsake us. God alone is the Comforter and Completer of our beings. He knows us inside and out...and loves us anyway.

About the Writers

Shae Cooke has contributed to over 40 books in both secular and non-secular markets. She works closely with international ministry and marketplace leaders, entertainers, writers, and publishers and travels North America to inspire people into the supernatural reality of relationship with God. She lives in beautiful Anmore, British Columbia, with her son, Jack Russell Terrier, and Wally Burger the Parrot.

Tammy Fitzgerald graduated from Cedarville University with a degree in English Literature and went on to become an editor at Destiny Image Publishing Company. She also recently completed her teacher's certification at Shippensburg University. She currently lives in Pennsylvania with her cat, and has her eyes open to see where in the world God will lead her next.

Donna Scuderi is a former high school English teacher and one-time rock musician who has been writing and editing professionally for more than a decade. Having served nine years in the editing department of an international ministry, she now serves a variety of individuals and organizations to perfect their message through print and public speaking. She also recently completed a feature-length screenplay.

Angela Rickabaugh Shears has been writing and editing for more than 20 years, although these Powder Room reflections are her first out-from-behind-the-scenes books. She earned her B.A. from the University of Hawaii Manoa with a major in journalism/communications and a minor in political science. Angela, her husband Darrell, and their Old English sheepdog Maggie, live in southcentral Pennsylvania...except when they are daydreaming about living back in Hawaii.